The Two Shall Become One

A 31-Day Devotional for a Stronger Marriage

By Dr. Greg and Suzanne Winslow

The Two Shall Become One:
A 31 Day Devotional for a Stronger Marriage

By Dr. Greg and Suzanne Winslow

Copyright 2017

Photography by Justine Leary
Back Photo by Josiah Winslow
Cover Design by gforgraphics.com

Copyright 2017. This publication may not be reproduced, stored in a retrieval system, or transmitted in any form or by any means – electronic, mechanical, photocopy, recording, or otherwise – without the prior written consent of the author.
A Codex Spiritualis Publication.
Printed in the United States of America.

ISBN-13: 978-1544784830
ISBN-10: 154478483X

Library of Congress data is available for this title.

FORWARD

I have known Greg and Suzanne Winslow for a decade and a half. My wife and I were missionaries in training under their direct and personal tutelages for over three and a half years. Their passion and love for our God Almighty, the Creator, flavors every aspect of their lives and they want to share this love with everyone.

In this time of unprecedented attacks on marriages and families, Greg and Suzanne have pressed into God's love for strong marriages that produce strong families. Home life and morals are disintegrating and man's love is failing, but they refuse to give in to the way of the enemy. This determination is what fuels Greg and Suzanne.

Read and listen to the wisdom and the simple solutions presenting God's way to marriage and family restoration. Love, God's love is the key that unlocks exactly what almost every couple dreamed their marriage would be, the joy of being husband and wife. Greg and Suzanne offer this for you to explore. Bon appetite!

William & Jane Rice Missionary, Pastor, Writer, Vagabonds for Hope

INTRODUCTION

"I loved the wedding, invite me to the marriage", the bill board said as we drove through Texas on our way back to Mexico. It was signed, "GOD."

I thought, "If there is a message this generation needs to hear it would be that one." Having officiated many expensive weddings and counseled many marriages, I've seen first hand where the priorities lie, in the wedding celebration, not the everyday life. It's our belief that God needs to be in the center of our lives and especially, marriages. Some put Him in the center of the wedding and that's as far as it goes.

However, God's plan for marriage mirrors His desire for His Son and the church, that they be one, and powerful here on earth. When the two are one they become a force to be reckoned with. Likewise, the marriage, when they both are one they are a force, a powerhouse for life and ministry.

Unfortunately, most have God on the outside looking in, as an "Emergency Room God;" one who we run to when things get too far gone and we've become desperate for anything. Most see marriage as having a helpmate, a companion, someone to spend life with, never realizing they were put together for so much more, to be a powerful reflection of Christ's love for His bride, the church.

Essentially the way I love my wife is the way I love God. It has been has said, "The way you do anything is the way you do everything." If we run our marriage sloppy, chances are our relationship with God, and everything else is a mess. Just about everything we do is an expression of what is on the inside.

This is a common verse I use at weddings: "For the Lord your God is bringing you into a good land, a land of brooks of water, of fountains and springs, that flow out of valleys and hills; a land of wheat and barley, of vines and fig trees and pomegranates, a land of olive oil and honey; a land in which you will eat bread without scarcity, in which you will lack nothing; a land whose stones are iron and out of whose hills you can dig copper." Deut 8:7-9.

These verses describe entering a new land, one previously not known, like entering into marriage. It flows with milk and honey, (all things sweet and good), and nobody would deny that marriage is sweet; we all love honey in marriage. However, the verse goes on to say that it also has copper and iron, strong useful stones you can build with, but require work to get them out of the ground. They are not just lying around for you to pick them up; you must work hard to mine them. Likewise, nobody would deny that marriage is work, but it is rewarding work when we take the time to mine the treasures that can be found there.

We believe this book helps you to dig down deeper to unearth the gems that will make your marriage amazing. Some of the tidbits that we have learned through our more than 30 years of marriage, we feel are important enough to share. We've had many bumps in the road, but staying together and flourishing is always God's plan for any marriage, so we knew we could make it to the other side. You have a family worth fighting for, gratefulness helps you to see that.

Investing in your marriage and family is the greatest investment you can make this side of heaven. My greatest desire is to walk into heaven with my wife and all my children and grandchildren, all accounted for because we made the investment in them, saw them as more important than any thing or event. You'll never regret the time you sow into them. What a man sows that will he reap. Make a decision to sow that precious commodity, time, into those you love the most. You'll be a happier, richer person as a result.

Greg & Suzanne

RAGING IN THE HOUSE

"The very next day a tormenting spirit from God overwhelmed Saul, and he began to rave in his house like a madman."
1 Sam 18:10 NLT

I found myself raging in the house like a madman. The next day I read this verse and realized that evil spirits got a hold of Saul and made him a madman. I saw the similarities and immediately took action by repenting. Then I renounced a spirit of anger, and took authority and cast it out. Immediately I had a change of heart. I got a lot calmer. Everything that had bothered me so much seemed to disappear, and the tension in the house I had caused, was broken.

Sometimes we need to understand, it's not my wife, it's not my husband, it's not the kids, it's the enemy. We've let him in one way or another, and now he's wreaking havoc in our marriage. It seems so easy to overlook the enemy as having his hands in our affairs, but he was the cause of the very first marriage problem, so he probably won't overlook my marriage either. I should understand this and take action accordingly. Many think they are exempt from attacks of the enemy, but he's probably more to blame than we think.

If you are experiencing more trials than usual, you might try redirecting your energy against the enemy, rather than your spouse. More than likely the enemy has managed to make an inroad and has you just where he wants. He likes people who show no resistance; or are unaware. Don't be one of them!

CONFESSION: I recognize the enemy's tactics and do not fall for them. I repent for allowing the enemy access in _____ area of my life. I renounce his activity in my life, kick him out, and determine to be more conscientious of his schemes against my marriage. Amen.

SECOND ATTACK

"Get ready for another attack. Begin making plans now, for the king of Aram will come back next spring."
1 Kings 20:22 NLT

One victory doesn't necessarily mean the end of the battle. In Israel, Ahab won a victory, but the first thing the Lord directed him to do was to not get comfortable because the enemy was already planning his next attack. When the enemy did attack Ahab again, he was met with a prepared army, one that had the backing of God, hence the enemy was defeated again. What happened? The king took the advice of the prophet and prepared. He didn't assume a time of peace meant the enemy wasn't thinking of a counter attack. As a result of being prepared the enemy didn't bother him anymore.

We're only more than conquerors when we recognize the provision God has given and act accordingly. Nothing is automatic. One must become engaged fully and sometimes for prolonged times where there have been specific areas of attack, but with God on your side, you can win if you don't give up. Many times throwing in the towel seems easier, but if you've won once you can win again. The word of the Lord teaches us how to win a counter attack as well. Implement a spirit of praise; become pro active in speaking life over your situation; set up a time when you can have effective communication. Ask yourself: How can I strengthen the weak areas so when the enemy tries to come at me again, he finds me ready and prepared?

CONFESSION: I am alert and prepared for the attacks of the enemy. I take into account my victory and take steps to insure it stays that way. The Word of God guides me to be aware of my enemy. I close the doors on his schemes in my life and in my marriage. Amen.

HE WHO FORGIVES ALWAYS WINS

But if you refuse to forgive others, your Father will not forgive your sins.
Matt 6:15

When I was president of the pastors alliance in Zihuatanejo, Mexico, a pastor really offended me by his comments. He gave me no credit as president of the alliance, nor as a pastor, neither as a Christian; so we stopped fellowshipping. When I would hear that bad things happened to him, inwardly I was glad, and felt like he deserved it. After some time the Lord spoke to me about asking him for forgiveness. I said, "Lord, *he* offended *me*. If he wants to talk, he can come to me. What he did to me was very offensive." The Lord spoke again and said, "Yes, but now your attitude is offensive to me." When He said that, I knew I had to go. I went to this pastors office and told him I was sorry because my attitude had become offensive to the Lord regarding him, and I wanted to make things right. Immediately he asked for forgiveness and in the spirit things were broken. I won: not the battle, but rather his friendship again. The situation was totally healed because I was willing to ask forgiveness. I have never seen asking for forgiveness fail when it is authentic.

If you've offended your spouse, it's impossible to have a healthy marriage with unforgiveness; it just won't happen. In the end if you were right about the argument, but lose the family, you were wrong. If there is one thing I've learned in all my years of being married it's this, "He who forgives, always wins." You don't necessarily win the battle but you win your marriage again. If there is offense, humble yourself, fix it, and win your marriage again.

CONFESSION: I am quick to forgive. I make it my business to be on good terms with everybody and hold no grudges, bitterness or offenses, especially against my spouse. Just as Jesus forgave me and commands me to forgive, I do so. I don't wait, I do it quickly. Amen.

NO RECORD OF WRONGS

"(Love) takes no account of the evil done to it [pays no attention to a suffered wrong]."
1 Cor 13:5 AMP

Reading this scripture can be difficult, especially if there is an abusive situation; yet love, God's love, which resides in us, keeps no record of wrongs. God does not have an account of things we've done wrong to Him, and we shouldn't have one with our spouse either. If we are going to walk in God's love we all will have to decide to overlook offenses. Offenses are offensive. They can hurt, they bruise, they wound, but love can heal them, if we don't have an account of them.

Think of the meaning of the word account. Like registering money that comes in or goes out, we know every transaction. An account of offenses keeps track of what and when things happen to us. This is the very opposite of love. Love has no offense registers, rather an ability to forgive those times and not remember, or even pay attention to them, as the Amplified Bible states.

Are you keeping an account of all the bad things done to you or the things that should have been done and were not? It's time to forgive and let it go, which is exactly what it means to walk in love. Walking in love is not some sweet emotion that makes me feel good. It's walking like Jesus did, who even on the cross forgave the very ones responsible for his pain. Being like Jesus means I will have to forgive people for their failures toward me, their actions and offenses. I would rather walk like Jesus than waste my time keeping an account and rehashing all they have done. My God is bigger; His love is in me, I can do it.

CONFESSION: I keep no account of wrongs done to me. I walk in God's love, keeping my heart pure, overlooking and forgiving offenses. I make quick decisions to forgive. Amen.

DETERMINED

"Love bears up under anything and everything that comes, is ever ready to believe the best of every person."
1 Cor 13:7 AMP

God is determined to love you, so shouldn't you be determined to love your spouse? If your marriage is important to God it should be important to you. This love, the love that God has given the Christian, speaks of a determination that doesn't move when negative things may come its way. Love has already made up its mind that it's going to stay strong through the storm. When things got rocky or stressed in our marriage we would look at each other and say, "God put us together; therefore, we can work through this." It was God's will that we be together, therefore, we can get over this hump." We never saw ourselves as anything besides being together, for life. We have, like many, weathered storms, always knowing that He has supplied us with all we need to get through every obstacle.

You have everything you need as well. God is for your marriage, even if it started off wrong. As tough as it might get, be determined to walk in this love that bears all things and believes the best. See your marriage as strong, even if it doesn't look that way. Stay positive! Stay in faith. Remember what David said when being persecuted by Saul, "I will bless the Lord at all times, his praise will continually be on my lips". He didn't feel like praising but he knew it would change things. He was a master of encouraging himself in difficult times. He kept his eyes on the all powerful God, for change, and it always came.

CONFESSION: Nothing comes in the way of me loving my spouse the way God loves me. I let that love operate and dominate my marriage. Amen.

WITHOUT WEAKENING

*"(Love's) hopes are fadeless under **all** circumstances, and it endures everything [without weakening]."*
1 Cor 13:7 AMP

You and I alike made a commitment to each other before God. This commitment brings all the backing of heaven to be able to stand strong under the most difficult of circumstances. Because it wasn't based on circumstances, circumstances can't destroy it, unless you allow them. That commitment will most likely be challenged more times than you want. However, that is where love becomes strengthened.

I used to be very interested in body building. We had a schedule to work different parts of the body on certain days. The area you worked on the day before had to have time to heal. Your biceps for example, are made up of many muscle fibers. When you work them by lifting weights they break, then they heal stronger. If they are never worked, they never get stronger. Likewise, with love, which more reflects a muscle than an emotion, when our love for each other is challenged and perseveres, it actually grows stronger.

The apostles rejoiced in hard times because they saw themselves strengthened rather than weakened by trials. They brought God on the scene by rejoicing, and the situation dramatically changed. Do you want to strengthen those faith muscles? Take a posture of rejoicing, the unwavering language of love.

CONFESSION: I do not weaken in my love commitment towards my spouse. My commitment stands strong as the day I made it. I'm determined to learn from obstacles, even rejoicing in them. Amen.

CHILDISH THINGS

"When I was a child, I talked like a child, I thought like a child, I reasoned like a child; now that I have become a man, I am done with childish ways and have put them aside."
1 Cor 13:11 AMP

Right at the end of the love chapter, 1 Corinthians 13, Paul speaks about putting away childish things. That's interesting. God's love hits hard on selfishness. Someone once told me, if you want to know how selfish you are get married; to know the depths of selfishness, have a child; and the more you have the more you see how selfish you are. I've had six and can attest to that. However, selfishness is childish, and the Lord calls us to put it away. If it's keeping you from loving, put it away. Banish childish or selfish talk and selfish reasoning, which is an enemy, although it feels natural to marriage. God's love for marriage, like God Himself, looks out for the other person and walks on fulfilled. Childish reasoning says, "What about me?" Thank God Jesus didn't say that. God's love gives, childish love takes.

When one becomes a man or matures, he does not continue childish ways. If we saw a grown person playing with trucks and dolls, we'd think something's wrong; those aren't for grown-ups. Likewise, a mature person should put away the childish self-centered love and move onto more mature love, one that looks out for others. Have you put away childish things? You're not throwing a fit when something doesn't go your way, are you? Time to put it away!

CONFESSION: I put childish things away, that childish way of insisting on my own way. I look out for my spouse and am fulfilled in meeting his/her needs. I know my needs will be met in doing so. Amen.

WE'RE ON THE SAME TEAM

"... and they shall become one flesh."
Gen 2:24 NKJV

Over the years, when things have gotten intense in our household, the one line that has always knocked us back into our senses is, "We are on the same team." It has knocked us back because it makes us see that it's not about me. It's not always about what I want, but what's best for the family. When you stop and think about it, we both want the same things. We both want a strong marriage, one that reflects Jesus. We both want strong children who love God, we both want a strong ministry, etc. Therefore it only makes sense to work together for what we both want, and not against each other. Who best to accomplish this with, than the one you've sworn to have and to hold throughout your lifetime? The way I see it, God put us together as a team, so we should work together as one. As a team we are more powerful to accomplish more. We each bring something to the table that the other could not. Team players want to win, not be the superstar.

We encourage you to stop pulling against each other and start working with each other, and a great place to start is to understand that you both should want the same basic things as a marriage and family. You're a team working for the same goals. If not, why not? Stop pointing the finger at each other and make it happen. Shake yourselves, like we've had to many a time and say, "We're on the same team."

CONFESSION: I thank God for my spouse, my greatest teammate. Together, we will have the same things: a great marriage, a great family, and working together we will glorify God in whatever we do. Amen.

SEX IS FOR PROTECTION

"But King Solomon loved many foreign women..."
1 Kings 11:1

People by nature are attracted to beauty. That's why many are attracted to God. Beauty is the overwhelming characteristic of all that God creates. It dominates heaven and is the reason that man is attracted to woman. Adam took one look at Eve, and it was all over for him; he was struck and in love. These days, flaunting beauty is how many people sell things. Men can easily be distracted by all this flaunting and need protection. This protection is provided by his wife. When my wife looks good, and she *always* does, she's protecting me. She's making sure that my eyes are only for her.

A healthy sex life is protection as well: protection of a man's self esteem, self worth, and security in his wife's love. While a woman might not feel the constant need like a man might, or understand fully what sex does for a man, essentially, she's protecting him from bombardment of the enemy. Granted, she should not feel like a piece of meat, or all she's worth is found in satisfying a man sexually, but a frustrated man is a bear to live with.

This is why the Apostle Paul says to not deprive one another of this gift. It's not a privilege, it's not something earned for good behavior. It's an expression, a holy expression of love towards one another and should always be kept in that regard. I have always compared it to worship, because in true worship is where you can bare your heart and show intimate love to our Savior. The same with intimacy with our spouses; the more authentic, the more focused it is, the better.

CONFESSION: I love my spouse with holy expressions. I am conscious of his/her intimate needs and meet them, knowing I am protecting myself and my marriage. We are healthy and active in this area. Amen.

COMMUNICATION IS THE KEY

"Phinehas the priest, all the heads of the congregation...heard what the Reubenites, Gadites, and the half-tribe of Manasseh had to say. They were satisfied...there was no more talk of attacking and destroying..."
Josh 2:30, 33

As pastors we've had to spend many a time in counseling sessions listening to one side then the other. By the time we finish listening to both sides usually I come to the conclusion that their situation is not that drastic, just a need to be heard. Nine times out of ten they ask forgiveness for being insensitive or something else, then leave on the mend. If they'd have taken a little time to do that exact thing on their own they wouldn't need us. However, many fail at this simple thing, to take the time to talk things out. Many just don't want to be bothered.

The fear or dislike of confrontation makes one prefer to continue with offense in their heart. Again, as a pastor I have had to, on many occasions, step outside of my comfort zone and confront people about things they are doing. It's difficult because you never know how the other person will react, but I have seen respect come to the person who can lovingly confront with the goal of straightening out crooked situations. In the above scripture, war was about to break out over assumptions. The looming war was not stopped until they took the time to listen to each other. Likewise in a marriage, when you take the time to communicate effectively, which is not accusing or attacking, then you too will win love and respect you deserve. No one respects lazy or irresponsible people! Step out of your comfort zone and take the time to communicate with your spouse. The TV, Facebook, are not that important, your spouse is.

CONFESSION: I take time to listen, because my spouse is important to me. I listen without attacking or accusing, I am not afraid to confront because I know it is for our best. Amen.

CHRIST MAKES ME COMPLETE

"... and you are complete in Him..."
Col 2:10 NKJV

Many people put their sense of worth in what other people say or think about them. They have a constant need to hear approval from men; however, the scripture clearly states that no one person makes us complete, only Jesus Christ. This can be a hard point to accept, but if we can, we can walk tall, knowing that regardless of what anybody says, thinks, or does, I am still accepted and loved by God. Nobody can change that, and my confidence should always be in the unmovable.

When I can get to that point of finding my worth in God's approval alone, I am truly free to love even people who mistreat me. Many hope their husband or wife can fill that void, only meant to be filled by God alone. When they fail to do so, emotions get wounded leading to all sorts of problems.

Early in my marriage I was told this very truth, that I was complete in Christ alone; however, I did not accept it. I was in love and had a very low self image, so I wanted my wife's approval. However, approval can be as up and down as a roller coaster, and if one depends on approval they are generally unstable because: performance down, approval down; performance up, my approval goes up. Thus any type of constructive criticism or suggestion was always seen as a threat, making me feel I wasn't doing good enough, which only fostered the insecurity. Christ makes me complete. My life depends on Him; before Him I stand. He is able to make me stand, not some person, nor even my spouse. Christ is my all sufficiency. When I understand this, when I stop arguing with this truth and believe it, I am maturing.

CONFESSION: God's Word declares I am complete in Him, therefore I believe it. I don't live for the praise of others. I am thankful for Him making me complete which makes me stand. Amen.

ARGUE NAKED

"Now the man and his wife were both naked, but they felt no shame"
Gen 2:25

My good friend Bill Rice wrote a great book about marriage called "Argue Naked." When he told me about it I gave him a strange look with suspicious eyes, however, as I read it, I understood that he was not so much talking about no clothes on as he was about nothing hidden, no secrets, no dark closets. Naked in Genesis 2, means just that, not an absence of clothing, although there was, but nothing to be in the way of communication; nothing in the way of their expressions of love and commitment; essentially nothing hidden.

When we argue we tend to point fingers, accuse, and exaggerate the truth, yet all those indicate that something is hidden: hurts, wounds, and the like making us unable to be transparent with each other, causing even more damage. Basically, if you can't be transparent with your spouse, then with whom can you be transparent? We feel we will lose something if we become transparent.

We have established two things we do when we communicate with each other: We never use the words "never" and "always," as they are accusative, untrue words. For example: "You *never* help around the house" or, "you *always* forget our anniversary." We set ourselves up for major problems using accusing and untrue terms like that, even when appearing valid. Accusing puts me in the devil's court, as he is "the accuser of the brethren." Correct communication does not accuse nor does it defend itself; it listens with the posture of fixing, not being right. Stay transparent, don't accuse or defend, be quick to forgive.

CONFESSION: I am quick to forgive. I do not accuse my spouse but am quick to listen, slow to speak and slow to anger. My goal in my house is to have peace, not be right. Amen.

DANCE

"Then David danced before the Lord with all his might"
2 Sam 6:14

Making time in this busy day requires a decision to make it happen. If we don't write it on the calendar it might never happen. Taking time to be together is a choice and when the devil sees it happen, he attacks with all he's got. Many times we are more interested in the distant friend we never see on Facebook than we are with the person who is committed to us and is right next to us. Some have "couch time," "tacos at ten," "wine at nine," "date night," whatever, the idea is to make and spend time with each other on a regular basis.

We decided to spend our mornings together. Praying and worshipping. We decided that the first fifteen minutes would be dancing before the Lord, rejoicing, unhindered and unashamed. We encouraged each other when the other was slow to get out of bed. We laughed at the sight of each other, sometimes in our PJ's, twirling about, we didn't care if it sounded good or not we wanted to rejoice, we needed to worship. When you do so, it makes the day so much easier, so much fun, so much lighter, and even more romantic. Take time to dance, take time to worship as a couple, take time together.

CONFESSION: We make time to seek God, to worship Him, to spend time together, as a marriage unit. We make it happen. We delight in each others presence. We are a source of encouragement to each other Amen.

COVER HIS NAKEDNESS

"One day he (Noah) drank some wine he had made, and he became drunk and lay naked inside his tent. Ham, the father of Canaan, saw that his father was naked and went outside and told his brothers."
Gen 9:21-23

Noah was in the wrong. He had gotten himself drunk and went around flaunting himself naked, then fell asleep uncovered. When Ham saw this, he used it as an opportunity to spread the news, even if it was only to family. Essentially he did not cover his fathers nakedness; he divulged it; he kept him uncovered. His nobler brothers walked in backwards to not see their father's nakedness and covered him, a true sign of respect and love, even though their father had fallen into error.

Many people don't want counseling because of this uncovering of nakedness of things done wrong. Sometimes counseling sessions are spat sessions when feeling the support of another, one spews all the things done wrong by the other, but the marriage vow is meant for protection. I understand some things need to be said to get help. I am not talking about that. I am talking about complaining about each other to other people, who might only gossip rather than help.

When we go around divulging mistakes, even though they are legitimate, all we are doing is uncovering our spouse. Curses and difficulty were brought upon Ham for doing so, but blessings upon the brothers who covered their fathers sin. I am not talking about living with an abuser. I am talking about complaining about spouses who make mistakes and can be helped back into line.

Noah felt the support of Japheth and Shem, but humiliation from Ham. It's not our job to divulge and humiliate, rather build up and edify. This can be a challenge to those whose best friend is their mother or father.

CONFESSION: I build up my spouse. I don't divulge his/her errors. I extend grace to them; God's not done with them yet. Amen.

ENGAGED

"And if a house is divided against itself, that house cannot stand."
Mark 3:25 NKJV

Engaged in the terms of marriage means two coming together as one to form a family. In terms of war, it speaks of all-in, full attention. When two are engaged, they are locked in to a certain assignment. Many come together to form a family but are not locked in, or start out locked in but become unlocked, or even worse, a house divided. A house divided, that goes in two directions, that fights against each other for different means, will surely fall. You can't go two different directions and stand strong. Somewhere along the way, you will have to refocus again. The problem is many times we just continue on, not realizing we're not on the same page, while our house is crumbling.

Our house is meant to be a testimony of how Christ acts with the church, how the bride responds to Jesus. The way we act towards our spouse is many times a reflection of how we act with Jesus. We think we're okay, we give ourselves extra grace, but really we're a divided house. How do we fix it? By working together and getting on the same page: same page about finances, same page about child training, same page about how you communicate with each other. Marriage is work.

Divisions will come if we do not become focused, especially knowing there is an enemy ready to pounce. Are you married but not engaged? If so, there are more than likely problems brewing. Make the decision: I'm all in, in this marriage: I'm going to take stands I should have long ago, I'm going to work together as one unit with my spouse.

CONFESSION: I am engaged and on the same page with my spouse. I will not allow the devil to create a house divided against itself. I take steps to put in order what has been disengaged. I am all in in my marriage. Amen.

TWO BECOME ONE

"This explains why a man leaves his father and mother and is joined to his wife, and the two are united into one."
Gen 2:24

When I read this account in the gospels where Jesus was talking about divorce, and He quoted the part where it said, "This explains why a man leaves his father and mother," I must admit, I didn't see the explanation. It can be hard to see; however, when the Lord brought all the creation to the man, no suitor was found for the man; however, when the woman was brought to Adam, he might have said something like this: "At last; a suitable helper with whom to become one to fulfill God's purpose".

God created man and woman, husband and wife in His image. That image is the unity the Godhead had when they decided to make man in the first place. Many times we think it's a three part man, body, soul and spirit, but I would submit that it was a unity in the Godhead that went on to make a powerful creation. There is something a man cannot do with his father, mother, or his siblings, only with his wife. That is why a man leaves his parents, to unify with his wife and become powerful in the land.

God puts us together for power. Think of Christ and the church. Christ works through the church to continue to destroy the works of the devil. The head and the body have the same powerful ministry. When I join to my wife, speak the same language, we become powerful in the earth like Christ and the church. We become unstoppable. This is why the devil looks to break up marriages constantly, because when unified, they become a force to be reckoned with. Become ministry minded in your marriage and watch the miracles happen.

CONFESSION: I am one with my wife. God has destined us for power, and when we walk in unity, we are powerful against the enemy. We are ministry minded and destroy the works of the enemy! Amen.

MINISTER TOGETHER

"Come, my beloved, let us go forth into the field; let us lodge in the villages. Let us get up early to the vineyards; let us see if the vine flourish, whether the tender grape appear, and the pomegranates bud forth: there will I give thee my loves."
Song 7:11-12

These verses not only talk about intimacy with the Lord but also his vision for the field and villages. It's what I like to call the missionary scripture, for the wife is invited to go to the fields and vineyards, check out its fruit, and take care of the tender shoots. This speaks of the wife joining the husband in field ministry. As a couple you are much stronger together.

There is a special love that goes on when the two are involved in ministry. Notice Solomon didn't ask another king or officials to join him, rather his beloved. My wife is my favorite person to minister with. When she's along side of me, I feel more confident, and I know that God will use us greatly. After the fact, when He does, we have a special time of sharing because we were both involved. We both get excited about the same things that happened, as opposed to just the one who ministered.

As a couple, look for opportunities to minister together. If you're in the company of friends that are sick, even if it's just a cold, ask to pray for them. Invite a couple over for coffee and make sure you pray for them before they leave. Don't let fear of what others think keep you from sharing the power you have. Be conscious of always being a blessing to others around you, because they are always believing for something, and you can join them in their faith. They will appreciate it more than you know. Make opportunities to minister together. Remember, together you are a force to be reckoned with.

CONFESSION: My marriage is a ministry powerhouse. We see and take advantage of every opportunity. We support each other in ministry. Amen.

HEALING WORDS

"And let us not neglect our meeting together, as some people do, but encourage one another, especially now that the day of his return is drawing near."
Heb 10:25 NLT

Usually when we think about the above verse, we think about going to church, and that's what it does mean; however, looking at it in light of marriage, it applies as well. Many families now do not meet regularly. They sit in front of the TV and call it doing something together. In reality they are focused on a screen that is talking to them, but there is no dialogue. It's like going to a restaurant with a TV on, that serves only to distract; however, this verse exhorts us to meet together and take the time to encourage each other, especially because the day of Christ's return is getting closer. What would our marriage look like if we actually did that?

Any time our family comes under much stress, we never ignore it, we never disengage by watching TV, we always call a family meeting to figure out what is going on. Usually by the end of a meeting, things are worked out, forgiveness asked, restoration accomplished, as we pray together, encouraging each other, whatever it takes.

In the verse above, it says to encourage one another daily while you are able. Once while I was visiting a family early one morning in Mexico, the man was getting ready for work, while he was talking to me. While talking to various people in the home, we started looking for the man. I asked the wife, "Where did Fernando go?" She said she didn't know. Come to find out, he had left for work, but he didn't say anything to anybody, especially to his wife. I thought, "How strange: no goodbye, no anything, what if he dies today and left without saying anything?"

Many of us are the same. We don't take the time, the few minutes to talk with our family, to assure them we love them.

CONFESSION: I take time with my loved ones. Amen.

BELIEVING CONTRARY

"But at midnight Paul and Silas were praying and singing hymns to God, and the prisoners were listening to them. Suddenly there was a great earthquake, so that the foundations of the prison were shaken; and immediately all the doors were opened and everyone's chains were loosed."
Acts 16:25-26

One of my favorite movie scenes is in "Singing in the rain." Every now and then I break out this scene to encourage myself. Gene Kelly says in the midst of a downpour, " I only see sun shining," then proceeds to dance and have a happy time in the middle of the storm. He's singing and stomping in puddles. Nothing is going to keep him from a good time, not rain, not storm, not anything. Toward the end of the scene a police officer comes up to him and gives him the look as if he is doing something wrong, but even that doesn't deter him, he just smiles and goes off, even giving his umbrella away to someone who doesn't have one.

The rain isn't keeping him from rejoicing. Don't let anything keep you from rejoicing either. When we sing in the rain, we slap the devil in the face and declare that God is bigger, the sun will come out again; this too shall pass. We can focus on the temporary and allow it to discourage us or see the big God and dance away. I think that was the secret that made the early church unstoppable. Beating them only made them praise louder; killing them only made them multiply; impossible situations only made the miracles more powerful. That's the same God we serve and He is for our marriage. Our God is for us.

Next time it rains I'll see you outside. I'll be right next to you stomping in the puddles.

CONFESSION: I choose to sing in the face of adversity. I am not moved by what I see or feel, only by the Word of God, and it says that God is for me, therefore, I can face and conquer situations because my God is for me. Amen.

TIME TO SOW

"...for whatever a man sows, that he will also reap"
Gal 6:7

When Suzanne and I were first married, we waited one year before having children, even though we were in our late twenties. We would escape every weekend or any chance we could to go off on our own just to be together. Any free time we had, we spent together, enjoying each other, wherever we were. Even though we made very little money at that time, we didn't allow that to stop us from sowing into each other.

The interesting thing is we never went hungry; we never missed the rent; nor did we ever go poor as a result. It was as if God blessed our vacation time, our sowing into each other time. I truly believe that God likes our taking time off to spend with each other. I'm not talking about irresponsibility; I'm talking about taking time to strengthen the most important relationship, next to the one you have with God. I believe he blesses that.

We know people that after years of being married will say to us, "We never had a honeymoon." As a young Christian I remember asking a gal who was a Christian, some advice for marriage. She said, "Always take a honeymoon, even if it's only for a weekend, never put it off," I thought to myself, "Who would do that?" yet over the years we've met plenty who have.

For our honeymoon I went to the opposite extreme and took two weeks. Our first year of marriage was great because we always sowed into each other. As the kids came we missed those times of being able to sow freely as before; however we have always taken time to go places and be with each other, especially when stress is high. In stressful times we sow into each other.

CONFESSION: We take time to sow into each other, we don't take it lightly. We spend quality time together, and enjoy each other . Amen.

UNITED FOR POWER

"Oh, that they were wise and could understand this! Oh, that they might know their fate! How could one person chase a thousand of them, and two people put ten thousand to flight"
Deut 32:29-30

Moses, giving his last message to God's people before he climbs the mountain and dies, says, "Oh," which is a deep exclamation of emotion. He desires that the people of God would be wise and understand this, that they would know their fate; which is a powerful strength because they are God's people. United, they are even greater; to the tune of one chasing a thousand, two chasing ten thousand. There is such a multiplication of power when two are agreed in warfare!

The only time you find God uniting people together is in marriage. "Oh," that we would be wise and understand: we are not put together only for family, only for children, only for helpmate, but for power. In a marriage we should be more ministry-minded, more kingdom-minded, have more understanding that we are here, just like the body of Christ is here, to make a statement to the goodness and power of God. A united marriage can push back the powerful onslaughts of the enemy. "Oh, that we would not be passive about the enemy when he attacks our family and our marriage. I believe the enemy knows the power that lies within a united marriage, which is why he dedicates so much time to try to divide it. May marriages understand that they are not weak, but rather a powerful force. The enemy should tremble with fear when he tries to touch family. The enemy is no match for a husband who joins with his wife in warfare prayer. He understands this, it's time we do too.

CONFESSION: I make the decision to join with my spouse in prayer for my family and the extension of the kingdom. We are united. We chase the enemy because we are more powerful together than separate. Amen.

GOD'S PROPERTY

"...and you are not your own? For you were bought at a price."
1 Cor 6:19-20 NKJV

Many times, especially at church, we go out of the way to help people. They never see us down, they never see us angry at them, we make sure of that. Whatever they need, especially new people, we go out of our way to make sure they have what they need, even at the cost of personal and financial sacrifice. This is not a bad thing; on the contrary it's a good thing and the right Christian attitude. We see these people as God's property, people whom God loves and died for, therefore we treat them as such.

What is it called when words and actions don't line up? For example, we become easily offended with our spouse and sparks fly. We tend to have choice words for *"our"* spouse, insults, pointing the finger, accusations fly such as, "You always this," "You never that." With the idea that she is, "just *my* wife," or, "He'll get my respect when he starts to take charge more spiritually;" seeing my spouse as God's property seems to go out the window. When we treat new people with more respect than the person we covenanted with, it shows disdain of God's property.

Your spouse is just as much God's property as is the person on the street. They deserve all your love and respect, just like you would show an unbeliever you want to win to the Lord. Your spouse is God's blood bought property, not your verbal punching bag, so treat them that way. Then you'll see God answer your prayers, then you'll see Him move you both into a better place.

CONFESSION: My spouse is God's own property, and I don't treat His property badly or speak carelessly of them, but with utmost respect and kindness. I keep this in mind as I walk it out. Thank you Jesus for my spouse. Amen.

ONE IN PURPOSE

"Look!" he said. "The people are united, and they all speak the same language. After this, nothing they set out to do will be impossible for them!"
Gen 11:6

When God said, "Let us make man in our image," many think He was talking about spirit, soul, and body. However, in the context of the verse, the Father, the Son, and the Holy Ghost were all in unity as to making man. The first image of God we see, is that of complete unity. Nothing is impossible to those who are in agreement. The tower of Babel demonstrates a powerful illustration of unity. Unity does the impossible. Unity defeats obstacles; it goes beyond what others, not unified, can do. When we are one in purpose, we will do what others cannot. This is why Jesus speaks over and over again about being in agreement. Actually faith is agreement or unity with what God has said.

When I declare the same, unity is there: nothing can be withheld, nothing will become impossible. When I am confused and speak a different language, I limit myself. Do my spouse and I speak the same language, have the same goals, the same vision? At first glance we do; however unity is revealed in my speaking, not my intention. I may have best of intentions, but that does not mean I am in unity. I may love my spouse, but that does not mean unity. Unity speaks and acts the same.

Another translation reads, "Nothing will be withheld from them." That is when mighty miracles happen, that is when advancement happens, that's when we become a force to be reckoned with. When we are on the same page, that's when we damage the devil's kingdom.

CONFESSION: We make the effort to be in unity. We are not going in two different directions. We are on the same page, and that makes us a powerful force to be reckoned with. Amen.

ONE IN SPEECH

"This fellow does not cast out demons except by Beelzebub, the ruler of the demons." But Jesus knew their thoughts, and said to them: "Every kingdom divided against itself is brought to desolation, and every city or <u>house</u> divided against itself will not stand."
Matt 12:24-25

The Pharisees accused Jesus of casting out demons by Satan himself, but in doing so they actually revealed Satan's tactics. We see it all throughout history and even at the crucifixion, when the nation divided, brought about death. A house divided cannot stand. It can't coexist; it *will* fall. This shows how important unity is to the success of anything we undertake. How can we prevail when we don't even speak the same language? Satan is a master at division. He uses it all the time and knows how to pit one against another. His success in this area is unprecedented, especially in the area of marriage, therefore, we have to rely on the strength of the Lord and make extra effort to do the things which strengthen unity.

Insisting on my way or right is a sure way to divide. When it's all about you, division is right behind. Wanting my space, wanting my way, wanting what I want will always divide. Marriage is for givers, not for takers. It is easy for one to think, "Do I have to do all the giving and never get anything in return?" That thinking is wrong, and marriage at its best should not work that way. It's in giving that we receive, even in marriage. When two think and speak that way, nothing shall become impossible for them.

CONFESSION: I speak in unity with my spouse. We both want the same things. We are not divided. We do not allow the enemy to pit one against the other, we recognize his tactics and refuse to cooperate with them. Amen.

COVENANT

"Let marriage be held in honor (esteemed worthy, precious, of great price, and especially dear) in all things."
Heb 13:4 AMP

God has made a covenant with us here on earth that will last throughout eternity. The only covenant similar is the marriage covenant. The people we covenanted with here will also be close to us in heaven. Family is God's idea, so is marriage. The aspect of family carries into eternity. We will not just die and disassociate ourselves from the people here we knew, especially family, therefore, we need to get along. I remember a time early in our marriage that Suzanne and I banged heads constantly. Everything was a situation. I made up my mind and said, "If I am going to be with Suzanne for the rest of my life (for divorce was never an option), I better learn to get along with her.." I determined to make sure I learned how to make amends quickly and have peace in the home. In our home being right was never the goal, peace was.

At one time we had a goal to see who would be the first to make up. That made situations in our marriage not last that long. We were not going to stay upset long, and especially not go to bed angry; that never happens and would have produced hardness of heart. Sweeping things under the carpet also produces hardness of heart. You willfully covenanted with your spouse. Start working that covenant to be stronger still. Covenant isn't till things get rough, it's for when things get rough. Covenant allows me to stand on my feet and make the right decision to continue on, like I said I would. In covenant, your word is everything, you gave it, now honor it.

CONFESSION: I stand by my word and what I covenanted to do, therefore God stands by me and my marriage as well. He does not leave in times of trouble, rather stays very close. We rely on Him and our path is straight. Amen.

RESPECT

"So again I say, each man must love his wife as he loves himself, and the wife must respect her husband."
Eph 5:33

Respect and honor all have to do with how I treat a person, and in family and marriage, respect and honor are exhorted to us by God. My biggest regret in life is how I treated my father with such disrespect. Because he wasn't a believer, I saw him as the enemy, and we would fight a lot. Finally the Lord dealt with me and spoke to my heart and said, " I have not called you to fight with your father, but to honor him and to love him." It was like a punch in the gut from God. However, I was grateful for it and determined to never have a strong discussion that would bring dishonor to him again.

As a matter of fact, when my dad was on his decline physically, three times I came to the United States to visit him and let him know that I loved him. I would not let him die and have regrets of not telling him I loved him. Praise God I was with him when he passed and I did have the opportunity with my other brother to lead him to the Lord months before he died. I thank God I was able to correct all the disrespect by determining to never be disrespectful to him again.

In marriage it is the same. We think because it's *my* wife I can treat her anyway I want, but it is not so. Spouses deserve our utmost respect. As scripture says, " Let marriage be held in honor" and again, "esteem others higher than ourselves." That's a great and rewarding thing to work on!

CONFESSION: I honor my spouse. We are not ordinary, rather extraordinary. As a result we esteem each other extraordinarily, with respect first and foremost. I am an example to my children in this area. Amen.

DON'T NURSE IT

"A fool shows his annoyance at once but a prudent man overlooks an offense."
Proverbs 12:16

If God tells us to overlook offenses, we couldn't possibly do so unless offenses come our way. Be expecting them. Be looking for them so you'll be ready to meet the challenge of looking right over the top of the them. When you look over the top, see Satan. Most of the time he's behind it anyway, so know that offense originates from the enemy. "For we wrestle not against flesh and blood but against principalities and powers etc.," Eph. 6:12.

Deep down, your spouse really does love you and doesn't want to hurt you. Love is always ready to believe the best; therefore, we must think the best; we must direct our thoughts to whatever things are true, honest, just, pure, lovely, of good report, if there be any virtue or praise. The offense that just took place between you and your spouse doesn't fit with this line of thinking, so stop thinking about it. When you overlook an offense you promote love, but if you repeat the matter, says Proverbs, you will separate close friends. Don't keep repeating the matter over and over in your mind. As you do, you are allowing the enemy footholds and roots, causing separation to go deep. Spouses are to draw near to each other, not become distanced. If your spouse is angry or the situation is too hot, you might need to separate from the person for a moment, till it cools down, and you can discuss the matter calmly. Anger provokes anger, and we can become entrapped in rage if we try to respond in the same anger being directed toward us. A kind word really does turn away wrath.

Don't nurse it, don't rehearse it, just disperse it.

CONFESSION: I don't rehearse offenses. I don't nurse them. I disperse all thoughts contrary to a healthy marriage. I set my mind on what is right. I thank God for my spouse. Amen.

THE POWER OF "I LOVE YOU"

"Now as the ark of the Lord came into the City of David, Michal, Saul's daughter, looked through a window and saw King David leaping and whirling before the Lord; and she despised him in her heart...Then David returned to bless his household."
2 Sam 6:16, 20

King David's marriage was on the rocks because He and his wife were going in two different directions. David wanted to go full throttle for the Lord. Michal wanted a nice dignified home that didn't necessarily include worship to God. When David had finished worshiping the Lord, he had it in his heart to bless his home. When he walked through the door he was met by his wife, who had stayed home from the celebration and began ridiculing him. She was going to set him straight and began making an issue over his actions. The blessing was changed to a curse and came back on her as she was never able to have children after that. She was essentially out of order. She was trying to conform David to her image, and he was having none of it. As spouses, as Christians, we are told to encourage each other daily.

The funny thing about encouragement is that it actually has a very positive effect on the hearer, and many times is reciprocal. Don't be afraid to encourage. Be afraid of not encouraging. Your words can produce life. If you don't believe me, look your spouse in the eye and say, "I love you" and see what happens. That's an encouraging word we all like to hear. Remember the song, "Home on the range"? Part of one verse says, "Where seldom is heard a discouraging word…" I want that to be my home's testimony. When I come home to bless the home, I want to be met with eagerness to receive, not reasons to keep quiet.

CONFESSION: I bless my home, and we receive encouragement and give it out. I determine that seldom is heard discouraging words in my home. Amen.

A CORD OF THREE STRANDS

"...And a threefold cord is not quickly broken."
Eccl 4:12

When the Bible talks about a cord of three strands, it's speaking of the husband, wife, and the Lord all intertwined together for the same purpose. It's hard to break such a combination, which is why the devil works so hard at it. Think of a rope of three strands. Separately they don't have much strength. They must be intertwined to become strong, which is what the word "abide" means in John 15 - intertwined. If one strand is removed, you cut your strength in half.

Think of a bone in your arm or leg. It is one bone. If it is broken, it becomes two bones and has no strength. To make it one again, it must be set and put in something stronger than the arm to keep it from moving around and healing in the wrong position. That cast is 1 Corinthians 13, the love of God, which He provides for each one of us. When we keep a record of wrongs, we are operating in something weaker and will set wrong.

When we don't believe the best, or when we do not forgive, we operate in something that will not hold us together, so we'll set crooked. Like unraveling a rope, our marriage becomes weakened, and if the bone sets wrong, we will always be unhappy or it will need to be broken again so we can heal correctly. Let the love of 1 Corinthians 13 be the cast that holds us firmly in place. It's the only thing strong enough to do so. Really, it all comes down to a decision to do it, and why wouldn't I want to if I want my marriage to glorify God? If need be, read 1 Corinthians 13 daily. Make it your confession, your declaration, your hope. That kind of love never fails.

CONFESSION: My marriage is strong because I allow the love of God to hold it together. I practice 1 Corinthians 13 and believe for the complete manifestation of that love to be evident in my marriage. Amen.

GRAN CAYMAN IS MOVING

Before I was married, I went on a Caribbean cruise. We were about three days into it and heading to the island of Gran Cayman. On a ship you tend to walk down the hallway bouncing off one side of the wall to the other, until you get your sea legs. I had finally gotten mine.

On the eve of arriving on Gran Cayman, much of the ship had gotten food poisoning. I was one of them. When we arrived at Gran Cayman, I was a bit woozy. The first thing I noticed, setting foot on Gran Cayman, was that the whole island was moving. I asked my sister if she felt that, too. She didn't. I tried to shrug it off, but the whole island was going up and down. What was happening? I had become accustomed to the rocky motion, so that stable ground felt unsure for me. I quickly headed back to what I thought was safety; the ship. My mind had me thinking that the small ship was more secure than that big island.

In marriage we can become so accustomed to rocky that normal feels weird. We've always been like this so we live on a small ship that gets tossed and turned by every wind and wave, instead of being a stable island. Don't become so accustomed to wobbly that solid feels weird. Solid is the norm in marriage, and that is what we should strive for. Regardless of what you see as how your marriage has always been, strive for the solid and firm. You might need to reject what you are feeling and declare, "This is not normal. I refuse to get seasick on land. I refuse to let my marriage end this way. We will finish strong."

Feelings are good, except when they convince you that you're in an unstable place when really you're not. See your marriage as God sees your marriage: Two as one.

CONFESSION: My marriage is solid. We trust in the Lord, and He makes our feet firm. We may feel like we are moving all over the place, but our trust is in Almighty God, and He is greater than what I see and feel. Amen.

BELIEVING THE BEST

"The Ammonite commanders said to Hanun, their master, "Do you really think these men are coming here to honor your father? No! David has sent them to spy out the city so they can come in and conquer it!"
2 Sam 10:3-4

The Ammonite commanders counseled their master wrongly because they didn't believe the best about king David's intentions. As a result he acted rashly, provoking one of the worst and most notable battles in David's life. They essentially provoked David into destroying them, and he did. Their rash actions brought on severe hurt and permanent damage to themselves. All of it could have been avoided if they hadn't listened to exterior voices. In our marriage we need to believe the best, as 1 Corinthians 13 says, "Love always...believes the best." If we start listening to the voice of suspicion, doubt or jealousy regarding our spouse, rough times are ahead.

When Suzanne and I were preparing for marriage, I was an extremely jealous man, I was very insecure. Every time I saw her talking to someone, my jealously would flare. I would think, "She's going to end up liking that person more than me," and my jealously would get the best of me, always causing problems with Suzanne. She was wise. She won me over by always affirming to me that I was the one, that she wasn't interested in another, that God put us together, that she loved me. After a while, I believed it, and jealousy was booted out of my life. It took some work on Suzanne's part, but she won by being consistent and patient with me. She always believed the best and taught me to do so as well.

CONFESSION: I believe the best of my spouse no matter what I see or feel. I affirm my spouse by saying that I love them and believe in them on a regular basis. I am not a jealous or suspicious person. I create an atmosphere of trust in my home by my constant affirmation of my love for my family. Amen.

DREAM AGAIN

"...And set me down in the midst of the valley; and it was full of bones. Then He caused me to pass by them all around, and behold, there were very many in the open valley; and indeed they were very dry. And He said to me, "Son of man, can these bones live?"
Ezek 37:1-3 NKJV

We meet so many people at the end of their rope with lost hope and shattered dreams. They've tried but still are in the same rut. I want to ask you, "Can you dream again? Can you see yourself in a better situation than today? Can you see yourselves with joy again in your marriage? Are you just hanging on till Jesus comes?" That's not God's best.

Ezekiel was taken to a valley of dry bones, excessively dry. God asked, "Can they live?" Under normal circumstances, all hope was lost, it was impossible. The prophet had a part to play in the miracle. He had to speak contrary. What he saw was dead and dry bones, unresponsive to anything except the power of God spoken through the man of God. When the prophet lined up with what God was saying, things began to rattle, things began to happen in the heavens, and things came together.

He had to speak a number of times, not just once, and even though he saw results after the first time, he still had to speak a second time. This is the same in our marriage. Keep speaking life over your marriage even though it might look like a valley of dry bones. God is greater, and when you line up with him, you will see movement. Stay at it, and it will become something that glorifies God again. Dream again! See yourself happy, blessed, ministering together. See a strong family, then speak it. Someone once said: "See it, believe it, live it!" Dare to dream again!

CONFESSION: I am not giving up on my marriage. I dream big. Nothing I am facing is bigger than God's ability to restore and make better my marriage. Amen.

GET READY

"You're not ready for this operation," the surgeon told me, "and I can't guarantee that your arm will straighten out anymore than it is. If anything, you might lose more."

I had broken my elbow the previous year and needed another operation. The first one left me with pain every day, no strength in my arm and I looked like a hunchback as my arm was locked at almost a 45 degree angle. The first doctor wanted to operate again but I had no confidence in him. Through a set of supernatural circumstances I now had an expert looking at my arm who thought he could fix the problem, but he wanted me mentally ready. I was exhausted from being in constant pain for a year and a half and I was ready. Everything was a go. I took his special appointment with a Chinese psychologist to prepare me, but didn't understand a word of it. I, "Yes sir'd," her to death. When the doctor came in the operating room he looked at me and asked, "Are you ready?" Already drugged I gave him a thumbs up and he said he was ready too. In recovery, physically I felt horrible, but I knew I was on the mend and felt better even though pain was racking my body. I began to praise God. Then I vomited.

During the following month of therapy, I told the therapist to ignore all grimaces on my face, not to go easy, I wanted my arm back. They did and every time I went to therapy I rejoiced because I was recovering. When I left, I left rejoicing. I became a praise machine praising God in pain, while being stretched, and seeing small results. Today I can stretch my arm 98%. I actually gained what the doctor said I might lose. I would not allow my arm to be crooked all my life. I set my mind to get it in order and I did.

I want to encourage you to have the same determination with your marriage. Get it back better than ever, get it straightened out straighter than ever, get it stronger than ever. Do like I did, become a praise machine when things look contrary. I praised God for little progress and praised God for big progress, in pain and not in pain. You can too. Like the doctor asked me, I will ask you, "Are you ready?" I know I was. I had had enough of pain and wanted healing, and I got it. Same rules apply to fixing anything. We get determined, we trust God's power to bring us through. I wanted it all my arm back, not just good enough. Scripture tells us that when Jesus went to Jerusalem to die on the cross, he set his face like a flint, meaning, he became determined that nothing was going to deter him from what needed to be done. Can you say, "Fresh Start?" Can you believe for restoration and miracles? Can you believe to be a powerhouse together, shaking the devil's kingdom like you were designed to do? It might be tough but if you keep at it God will honor you and bring things around.

If this book has helped you, read it again until the information isn't information anymore, but life. Most people think their situation is the exception, but God is God; He either can fix it or not. He waits for our cooperation. When we line up with Him things straighten out. We are believing with you for rejuvenation and to be taken to new levels, levels you never thought would happen. Even if you have a great marriage we want to believe that God would use your marriage even more. I know there is a definite shortage of role model marriages and we want to believe with you for yours to shine, as it was destined from the beginning. The world needs to see it. Your children need to see it, you need to walk it out.

Greg & Suzanne

WHAT'S YOUR ADVICE?

At some of our marriage nights we put up a piece of vinyl on the wall, calling it the advice wall, and asked people to write on it their best advice that they have learned in their marriage with the number of years they have been married next to it. So we thought we'd put that here as an extra. Below is what they've learned in their years of marriage, be those years many or few. What would you write on the wall?

*Stay strong and appreciate each other. (20 years)
*Buckle up and enjoy the ride. (18)
*Support and build your wife's self-image. Compliment, compliment, compliment. Tell your wife she's hot, and think it too.
Do something you wouldn't normally do. Have fun and be spontaneous. (7)
* Listen. (3)
*God's love never fails. (40)
*Honesty, patience, forgiveness. (4)
*Keep the line of communication open; respect each other. (48)
*Keep God in your marriage, and nothing is impossible to handle. Love joy, and peace. (23)
*Respect and communication. (7)
*Always be on the same page. (51)
*For-give– be <u>for</u> each other, <u>give</u> to each other; always forgive (26)
*Remind each other we're on the same team. (30)
*If in a disagreement, louder doesn't mean your right. (17)
*Forgive each other's flaws. (12)
*Respect each other; always speak in love, even during the hard times, always, always kiss. (15)
*Find contentment in the things you have, communication is the key.(9)
*Respect each other. (51)
*Build trust and protect it. (33)
*Believe that the Lord has put us together and will keep us together. (10)
*Deliberately pay attention to each other; communicate. (24)
* It's never too late to forgive.
*Keep God in the center; it will last. (10)

*Laugh with each other every day. (5)
*Your choice of words and tone of voice are very important.
*Let your last words be "I love you" whenever you part company, even if its texting or talking on the phone or just running errands. (16)
*3 f words– Forgive, Forget, go forward. (38)
*Let your no be no, and your yes be yes. (16
*Honor the husband, make the wife feel secure. (25)
*He who forgives always wins. (30)
*Never stop loving, forgiving, and communicating. (38)
*Jesus your center, Grace in truth, love in light, forgive and forget, Holy Spirit led, Trust in God the Father. (4)
*You cant change your spouse. It must be done by God. (18)
*Love unconditionally. (18)

CONTACT INFORMATION

If this book has been a blessing to you let us know, we'd love to hear from you. If you'd like additional copies of this book or to keep up to date with all that is going on with the Winslows, or if you would like to schedule a meeting with us at your church or function contact us at:
gpwinslow@hotmail.com

We'd love to come and minister. Look us up on Facebook.
Greg Winslow
Hidden Manna Ministries

Made in the USA
Middletown, DE
03 August 2021